Quick Tricks
for Learning

by Barbara F. Backer
illustrated by Marilynn G. Barr

To my mentors and teachers who led the way, and to Don who has encouraged every step of the journey.

Publisher: Roberta Suid
Design & Production: Standing Watch Productions
Cover Design: David Hale

Monday Morning Books
P.O. Box 1680
Palo Alto, CA 94302

E-mail us at: MMBooks@aol.com
Visit our Web site: www.mondaymorningbooks.com
Call us at: 1-800-255-6049

ISBN 1-57612-143-7

CONTENTS

INTRODUCTION

This book contains many "quick tricks"—activities that help children learn a variety of skills. The tricks show how to transform materials that are close at hand into intriguing learning materials and props for educational play. These tricks are designed around children's interests. Preschool children learn best from hands-on experiences with learning materials. Therefore, your children will be encouraged to talk and be excited about learning.

Enjoy the activities in a casual, informal setting and atmosphere. The emphasis is on having a thinking and learning experience, not in getting a correct answer. If your children offer incorrect information, ask them how they figured that out, and suggest other ways to explore. Remember that young children's brains have not finished developing. They are concrete thinkers and their way of looking at things is different from adults' methods. Children build their knowledge and their problem-solving abilities through repetition of activities like those in this book.

Everyday materials and your enthusiasm are all that are needed for these quick tricks. Your children will enjoy helping gather materials. Only a few activities require advance preparation. Some tricks call for the use of photos. With digital cameras and computer printers, making paper copies of photos is inexpensive and easy. Or use processed photos from other cameras. Make photocopies of these pictures and then use the inexpensive photocopies in the activities. Some copy machines will enlarge or reduce copies, which is convenient for some of the tricks in this book.

Use these quick tricks in any order. Relax and enjoy the time you spend doing the activities with your children. You will see their skills grow and their thinking and reasoning skills expand while together you delight in the fun of exploring and learning.

Throughout the book, *he* and *she*, *him* and *her* appear in different activities.

Barrettes, Barrettes
A Quick Trick with Paper Plates and Barrettes

Gather These Materials:
markers
several heavy-duty paper plates
14-inch (35 cm) lengths of bulky yarn, six for each plate
stapler and staples (for adult use only)
assorted plastic barrettes

Where: anywhere

How: Ask any child to use the markers to draw a face on a
paper plate. Gather three pieces of the yarn, hold them by
one end, then tie them together in a knot at that end of the
bundle. From this knot, braid three strands of yarn into one
braid, tying a knot at the bottom of the braid to hold it tight.
Repeat with the remaining yarn, making another braid. Staple
a braid to each side of the plate face. Repeat with more
plates, making several faces with braids.

Put the faces and a container of barrettes in a basket.
Show the children how they can put barrettes on the braids
and remove them, returning the barrettes to the container.
After they've had many opportunities to play with the activity,
encourage them to put a matching pattern of barrettes on
each braid.

Variation:
Let the children braid the yarn hair themselves.

Note:
A hot glue gun can be used instead of a stapler. Do this
away from the children.

This activity helps children learn about:
increasing small motor control, following directions, creating
and repeating patterns, braiding, and observing.

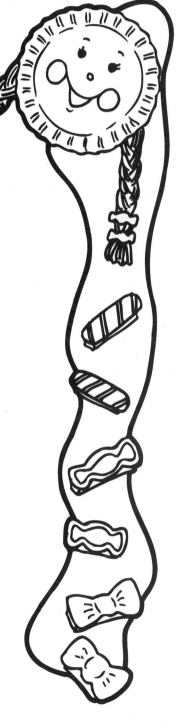

Half a Mask
A Quick Trick with A Paper Plate

Gather These Materials:
markers
white paper plates
scissors
glue
assorted craft items (construction paper, paints, crayons, feathers)
stapler and staples
drinking straw

Where: at a table

How: With a marker, draw a line across the center of a paper plate. Have the child cut the plate in half and use one half for a mask. Help him make a mark at the halfway point along the straight edge of the plate and cut a small semicircle at that point. This opening in the mask will rest on his nose. (Assist children who need help.)

Hold the plate half, curved side up, over the upper part of the child's face, with the opening resting on his nose. Have the child use his fingers to indicate where his eyes are. With a marker, make a mark at those two points on the plate. Remove the plate from the child's face and cut an eyehole around each mark.

Have the child decorate the mask with the assorted craft items. Suggest hair, eyebrows, animal stripes, ears, robotic features, and more. Help the child staple a drinking straw along the side of his mask. Show him how to hold the mask in place while using the straw as a handle.

Variation:
Have children make up impromptu scenes while "wearing" their masks. Talk about ways they can change their voices and movements to take on their new identities.

This activity helps children learn about:
engaging in dramatic play.

Quick Tricks for Learning ©2001 Monday Morning Books, Inc.

Zoom, Zoom
A Quick Trick with a Paper Plate

Gather These Materials:
white paper plates cut in half (half a plate for each child)
black paper
glue
markers
child-safe scissors
construction paper scraps
chart

Where: at a table to make the cars

How: Cut the black paper into small circles. (These will be the wheels on the paper plate cars.) Give each child half of a paper plate and two black circles. Have children turn the plates so that the straight edge is on the bottom. These plates will become cars. Have children glue the black circles on the straight edge for wheels, then have them use markers or construction paper scraps to make features for the car. They might add car doors or a driver and passengers. Some may color the entire car. Encourage all efforts.

Write the words to this song on a chart. Have children move their cars around while they sing the song. Use the chart as desired for language activities.

> Tune: "Twinkle, Twinkle, Little Star"
>
> Zoom, zoom goes my little car,
> Riding near and riding far.
> Around the curves, around the bend,
> Up the hills and down again,
> Zoom, zoom, goes my little car,
> Riding near and riding far.

Variation:
Encourage the children to make up more words to the song, telling other places the car goes. For more variety, have them substitute names of other vehicles for the word "car."

This activity helps children learn about:
rhythm and rhyming sounds and names of vehicles.

Framed!
A Quick Trick with a Plastic Plate

Gather These Materials:
children's artwork
sturdy plastic disposable plate with a rim (one for each child)
marker
scissors (for adult use only)
child-safe scissors
white glue
yarn
tape

Where: at a table

How: Collect children's artwork that you wish to frame. Place a plastic plate on a piece of cardboard larger than the plate. Trace around the plate's bottom. Cut the cardboard just inside the traced image, making a piece that fits inside the plate. This is your template.

Position the template over a piece of artwork and trace around the template. Have the artist cut on the line, trimming the artwork to fit inside the plate's bottom. Spread a thin layer of white glue inside the bottom of a plate and help the child lay the artwork atop the glue, with the art showing. Let the glue dry. Help the child tape a loop of yarn on the back of the plate at the top. Hang the artwork in a gallery display.

Variation:
Leftover plates from seasonal parties and birthdays make bright frames.

This activity helps children learn about:
valuing their work and displaying it with pride.

Quick Tricks for Learning ©2001 Monday Morning Books, Inc.

Colorful Flowers
A Quick Trick with Paper Plates

Gather These Materials:
small, white paper plates (one for each child)
markers or paints and paintbrushes
child-safe scissors
green construction paper
glue
permanent marker
colorful classroom items in a basket (more items than children)

Where: at a table to make the flowers
on the floor to use the flowers

How: Give each child a small plate and have him color it one color using a marker or one color of paint. Provide green construction paper and scissors, and have children cut out stems and leaves for their flowers. Have the children glue the leaves to their stem and the stems to their flowers. With a permanent marker, write each flower's color name in the center of the flower.

Spread the flowers on the floor. Pass the basket of colorful items and have each child select an item. In turn, let each child tell the color of his item and place the item on the matching color flower. Repeat the activity as long as it interests the children.

Variation:
For older children who are beginning to recognize letters and words, write each color's name on an individual index card. Make a card for each flower. Have each child select a color name card and place the card on a matching flower.

This activity helps children learn about:
learning and using color names.

Stick Puppets
A Quick Trick with a Lunch-Size Paper Bag

Gather These Materials:
child-safe scissors
magazine/catalog pictures of people or animals
glue
discarded file folders
lunch-size paper bags, one for each child
masking tape

Where: at a table

How: Have the children cut pictures of people or animals from magazines and catalogs. Have them glue their pictures onto file folder material. When the glue is dry, have children trim their pictures. These will become the tops of stick puppets.

Help each child roll a lunch-sized paper bag from one long edge to the other. Help her wrap masking tape around each end of this roll. This forms a stick or rod that can be used as the puppet's handle. Help her tape or glue the puppet shape onto the handle. Encourage small groups of children to create a simple show with their puppets.

Variation:
Have children use construction paper, markers, scissors, glue, and other art materials to make puppet parts (arms and legs) to glue to the paper bag sticks.

This activity helps children learn about:
making their own toys and learning materials.

Fabulous Flags
A Quick Trick with a Grocery Bag

Gather These Materials:
large grocery bags
scissors (for adult use only)
variety of art supplies including glue
rubber bands (two for each child)
masking tape

Where: at a table

How: For the flags, cut the bags to form large sheets of grocery bag paper. Trim away ragged edges and cut off the bottom of the bags, yielding a large rectangle. Cut these rectangles in half, crosswise and lengthwise, yielding four smaller rectangles. For the flag poles, cut just the bottom from the remaining bags and refold these bags, reserving them for later.

Give each child a small rectangle and a variety of art supplies. Challenge the children to make flags. When the flags are ready, help children attach them to sticks, which they make as follows:

Give each child a bottomless paper bag. Leave these folded flat. In turn, help each child roll a bag from one long edge to the other. While the child tightly holds the roll, wrap strips of masking tape around each end of the roll, forming a long, thin stick. Use additional tape or glue to help the child attach the flag to the stick. When items are dry, put on music and have the children march around with their flags.

Variation:
Use lunch-size bags to make hats for the band members. Let the children decorate the bags and then wear them upside-down on their heads.

This activity helps children learn about:
finding new uses for familiar items.

Paper Balls
A Quick Trick with Paper Bags

Gather These Materials:
lunch-size paper bags (one or more for each child)
newspaper
masking tape

Where: anywhere

How: Have each child open a lunch-size paper bag. Give each child a sheet of newspaper and have children do the following: Crumple the paper into a tight wad. Stuff the newspaper wad into the bottom of the paper bag. Twist the top of the bag closed and fold the twisted top over onto the stuffed part of the bag. While the child holds the bag, wrap masking tape around the stuffed bag to form a ball.

Variation:
Use large grocery bags to make large balls. Children enjoy using these for kicking activities and for soccer-like games.

This activity helps children learn about:
large motor coordination and reusing familiar objects in new ways.

Baseball Bats
A Quick Trick with a Grocery Bag

Gather These Materials:
large grocery bags (one for each child)
masking tape

Where: at a table or on the floor

How: Lay a large grocery bag flat on the table with the flap on top. Show the children how to roll the bag into a tight stick shape by starting at one long edge and tightly rolling to the other long edge. With each child in turn, help the children roll their bags. Have the child hold the rolled bag at each end while you wrap masking tape around the middle and at each end. Children can use their bats with Nylon Balls (see p. 87) or Paper Balls (p. 12).

Variation:
Encourage the children to experiment with other ways to use the paper bats. Encourage the children to make up their own games.

This activity helps children learn about:
large motor coordination and hand-eye coordination.

A Mouse and a House
A Quick Trick with Construction Paper

Gather These Materials:
mouse and house patterns (p. 15)
colored paper
crayons or markers
child-safe scissors
yarn scraps
tape
glue

Where: at a table

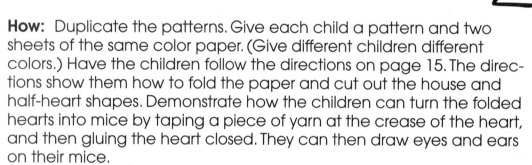

How: Duplicate the patterns. Give each child a pattern and two sheets of the same color paper. (Give different children different colors.) Have the children follow the directions on page 15. The directions show them how to fold the paper and cut out the house and half-heart shapes. Demonstrate how the children can turn the folded hearts into mice by taping a piece of yarn at the crease of the heart, and then gluing the heart closed. They can then draw eyes and ears on their mice.

All children put their mice and houses in a basket, making a color matching game. To play the game, children spread the houses on a flat surface, and then place each mouse on a house of the same color.

Variation:
Use the children's mice for a math bulletin board. Make five large mouse houses and number them 1 to 5. Put these on the bulletin board. Give children pieces of tape and have them arrange their mice so the correct number of mice surrounds each house.

This activity helps children learn about:
making their own learning materials and matching.

Mouse and House Patterns

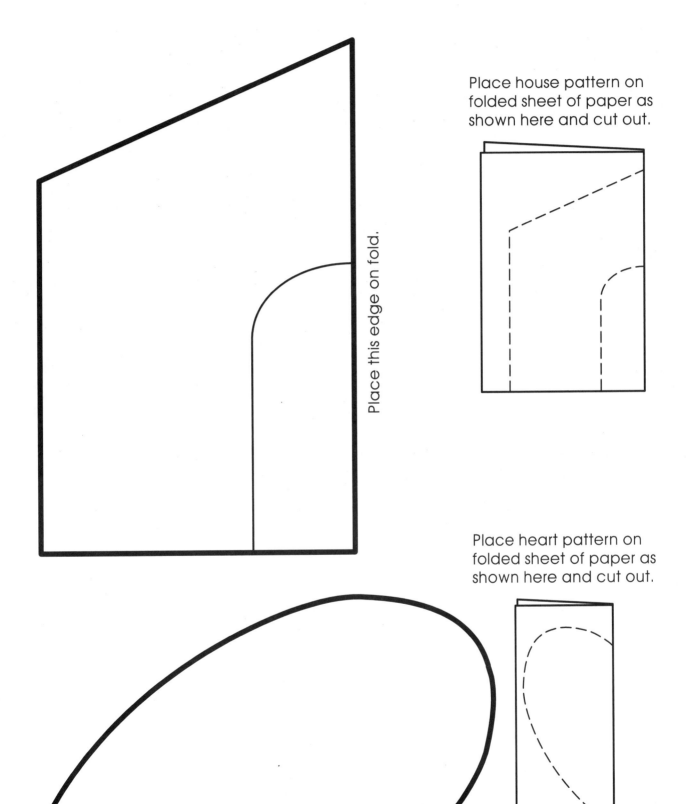

Place this edge on fold.

Place house pattern on folded sheet of paper as shown here and cut out.

Place heart pattern on folded sheet of paper as shown here and cut out.

Place this edge on fold.

Scampering Mice
A Quick Trick with a Paper Mouse

Gather These Materials:
paper mice from activity on p. 14

Where: anywhere

How: Each child holds his paper mouse. Children say (or the adult reads) the poem below, and the children help their mice act out the poem.

The mouse goes up, *(Mouse goes up child's arm.)*
The mouse comes down. *(Mouse goes down the arm.)*
The mouse likes to scamper
Across my crown. *(Mouse scoots across the child's forehead.)*

The mouse goes here, *(Child moves mouse anywhere.)*
The mouse goes there. *(Child moves mouse anywhere.)*
The mouse likes to scamper
Under a chair. *(Child puts mouse under a chair.)*

The mouse goes up
And sits on my head. *(Child moves mouse to his head.)*
Then he slides down my arm *(Mouse slides down arm to hand.)*
And into his bed. *(Child cups mouse in his palm.)*

The mouse goes to sleep.
The mouse starts to snore. *(Children make snoring noises.)*
When he wakes up tomorrow
We'll play some more.

Variation:
Have children use words indicating *position* (*near, far, left, right, inside, beneath*) to suggest places their mice can go. Have all children listen carefully and help their mice act out the suggestions.

This activity helps children learn about:
listening for details.

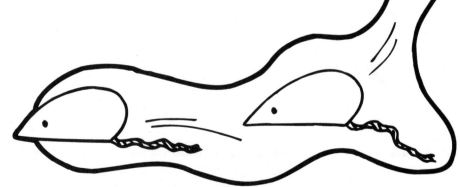

Matching Mice
A Quick Trick with Index Cards

Gather These Materials:
16 index cards
markers in eight colors plus black
clear, adhesive-backed paper (optional)

Where: at a table to make the game cards
at a table or on the floor to play the game

How: To make the game, draw one mouse on each index card. Color the mice, making one pair of mice for each of the eight colors. Use the black marker to add features to the mice. (Children can make these cards. The mice don't need to be identical. The important thing is to have two of each color.) If desired, cover the cards with clear, adhesive-backed paper for durability.

To play the game, two or three children spread the cards face down. In turn, a child turns two cards face up. If the cards match, the child captures them as his own. If they don't match, he turns them face down and leaves them in their original positions. Play continues until all pairs have been captured.

Variation:
For more difficulty, make four cards of each color. As before, children look for matching pairs, turning only two cards at a time. There will be two pair of each color.

This activity helps children learn about:
visual memory and taking turns.

Give a Mouse a Donut
A Quick Trick with Donut-Shaped Cereal

Gather These Materials:
markers
sheets of paper or poster board (one sheet per child)
small dish for each child
donut-shaped cereal (or any cereal)

Where: at a table

How: Have each child draw one mouse on his sheet of poster board. Give each child a small dish of donut-shaped cereal. Use the "donuts" to act out simple stories that introduce addition and subtraction concepts. Have children clear the mouse boards between each story by putting the remaining donuts back in the bowls or by eating the donuts. Keep the boards so you and the children can repeat the story activity on other days.

Sample stories:
1. The mouse found two donuts. (Children put two cereal pieces on their mice.) He ate one donut. (Children eat one of those pieces.) How many donuts were left? (Children count their cereal pieces.)
2. Mrs. Mouse gave the mouse one donut. (Children put one cereal piece on their mice.) Sister mouse gave him three donuts. (Children put three more cereal pieces on their mice.) How many donuts did he have? (Children count their cereal pieces.)
3. The mouse found three donuts by the slide. (Children put three cereal pieces on their mice.) He gave two donuts to the birds. (Children move two cereal pieces back to their bowls.) He ate one donut. (Children eat one cereal piece.) How many donuts were left? (Children count their cereal pieces.)

Variation:
After children have learned the routine, let them make up number stories using the mice and the donut-shaped cereal.

This activity helps children learn about:
listening for details and beginning to understand word problems.

Any Body
A Quick Trick with Magazine or Catalog Pictures

Gather These Materials:
magazine ads or catalogs with slick paper
scissors (for adult use only)
glue stick
plain paper (two or more sheets per child)
markers or crayons

Where: at a table

How: Cut pictures of full pieces of clothing from catalogs or magazines. (Do not use pictures of folded clothing.) Suggestions: slacks, shirts, sweaters, dresses, skirts, hats. Glue one piece of clothing to the center of each sheet of plain paper. Give a paper to each child and challenge the children to use markers or crayons to draw what is missing from the picture. Most will add complete body figures (heads, arms, legs, any missing torso) and some missing clothing. Encourage all efforts. Have the children show their finished pictures to each other and to talk about what they did.

Place any remaining unused sheets in the Art Area where children can repeat the activity as desired.

Variation:
In magazines, find large, close-up pictures of faces. Cut out the eyes, noses, and mouths from these pictures. Glue one facial feature onto each piece of paper. Have children use markers or crayons to add what's missing.

This activity helps children learn about:
naming body parts, observing for details, and part/whole relationships.

Houses and Homes
A Quick Trick with Paper and Crayons

Gather These Materials:
white drawing paper (one sheet per child)
crayons and markers
thumb tacks
paper scraps
glue

Where: at a table

How: Give each child a sheet of paper. Tell the children that they will each make a house. Show them how to fold the paper in half, crosswise. Have them place the paper in front of themselves with the fold at the top. Show how to fold the top corners of the paper so they meet in the paper's center, forming a peak for a roof.

Have them decorate their houses with windows and doors. Now have them open the roof flaps and draw items inside the flaps that might be seen in the attic. Have them unfold the papers, opening the house. Have them draw pictures of what might be inside the homes.

Gather the folded houses and mount them on a bulletin board by pushing a thumbtack through only the back layer of paper. Visitors to the board can unfold the houses to see what's inside. Encourage children to use paper scraps, markers, and glue to make trees, shrubbery, people, pets, vehicles and more for the bulletin board neighborhood.

Variation:
Children can spread their houses on the floor, creating a neighborhood. They can add building blocks and small vehicles.

This activity helps children learn about:
representing real things and the concepts of inside and outside.

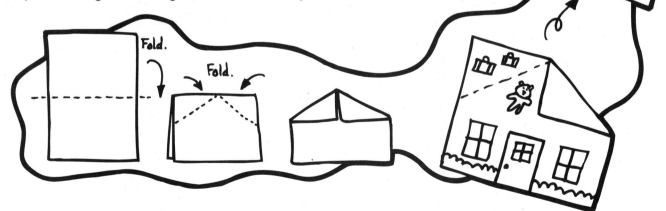

Quick Tricks for Learning ©2001 Monday Morning Books, Inc.

Newspaper Treasure Hunt
A Quick Trick with the Newspaper

Gather These Materials:
plain paper (one sheet for every two children)
marker
newspapers
scissors
glue sticks

Where: at a table

How: On each piece of paper, make a grid with eight squares. In each square of each grid, write or draw something that can be found in the newspaper, such as a letter, a numeral, a sight word, a house, a car, a picture of a sun or moon. Have children work in pairs. Give each pair a grid page and make newspapers available to them. Challenge children to find their items in the paper, cut them out, and glue them into the proper grid squares.

Variation:
This is a good activity for parents and children to do together. If needed, send newspaper pages home with the children.

This activity helps children learn about:
the newspaper, working together, and looking for details.

Paper People
A Quick Trick with Magazine or Catalog Pictures

Gather These Materials:
magazines and catalogs with slick paper
scissors (for adult use only)
glue stick
poster board
clear adhesive-backed paper

Where: at a table

How: From catalogs and magazines, cut out pictures of people.
Glue these onto poster board or recycled cardboard from cereal
boxes. Then cover with clear adhesive-backed paper, and trim away
the extra cardboard.

     Place these people in the Block Area where children can
incorporate them into block play. Or place the people in a container
with doll house furniture or small building blocks where children can
build scenarios around the characters.

Variation:
Cut out pictures of animals, cars, and furniture to use in the same way.

This activity helps children learn about:
incorporating props into dramatic play.

Quick Tricks for Learning ©2001 Monday Morning Books, Inc.

Terrific Telescopes
A Quick Trick with Index Cards

Gather These Materials:
index cards (one for each child)
masking tape

Where: anywhere

How: Have the children work in pairs. Each pair makes two telescopes. One child rolls an index card into a tube shape and holds the tube closed. The other child wraps strips of tape around the tube to keep it closed. Children switch jobs to create a second telescope.

While sitting in a group, challenge the children to use their terrific telescopes to find an object you describe, such as "something red" or "something made of wood," or "something alive." When a child tells what he sees, the group sings this song, inserting the child's name and the found item's name in the blanks:

> Tune: "The Farmer in the Dell"
>
> (Child's name) sees a _____.
> (Child's name) sees a _____.
> Lucky me, I see it too.
> We all see a _____.

Variation:
Let the children take turns sighting something with their telescopes and describing it (not naming it) for others to find.

This activity helps children learn about:
listening for details and using visual skills to find an item.

I see a plant.

Pointy Puppet
A Quick Trick with an Envelope

Gather These Materials:
envelopes (one per child)
markers
child-safe scissors

Where: at a table

How: Have each child open the envelope flap and place the envelope front-side-up on the table with the flap's point facing his body. This becomes the puppet's head, and the point can be a nose, beak, beard, chin or whatever the artist imagines. Have the child use markers to add the puppet's features. The child then sticks his hand inside the envelope to animate the puppet.

Encourage the children to make puppets of imaginary animals, and then have them tell about their animals and demonstrate the noises their animal makes.

Note: Experiment with different sizes of envelopes

Variation:
For a puppet with large ears or with horns, have the child use scissors to cut two holes in the envelope's top folded edge. Have him stick his fingers through the holes to give his puppet ears or horns.

This activity helps children learn about:
language and vocabulary development.

Quick Tricks for Learning ©2001 Monday Morning Books, Inc.

A Pattern of Friends
A Quick Trick with Familiar Photos

Gather These Materials:
individual close-up photos of two classmates
scissors (for adult use only)
glue stick
40 index cards
clear, adhesive-backed paper

Where: at a table to make the game
anywhere to play the game

How: Make 20 identical copies of each photo. Trim the photos to fit onto index cards. Glue each photo to an index card and cover each card with clear, adhesive-backed paper for durability. Use the cards to demonstrate patterning activities. Challenge the children to make an A-B-A-B pattern with the photos. Place the photos where children can play with them at will.

Variation:
Use the cards to demonstrate an A-A-B-A-A-B pattern or an A-B-B-A-B-B pattern and challenge the children to make these patterns with the photos.

This activity helps children learn about:
predicting what comes next.

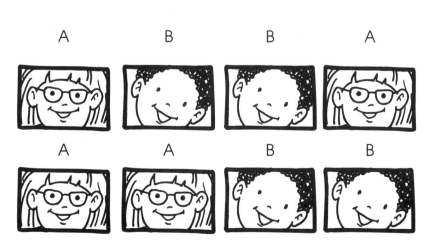

A	B	B	A

A	A	B	B

A Puppet That's Me
A Quick Trick with a Child's Photo

Gather These Materials:
a paper copy of a photo of each child (see pg. 4)
child-safe scissors
cardboard
glue stick
clear, adhesive-backed paper
scissors (for adult use only)
large or small craft sticks (one per child)
stapler and staples

Where: anywhere

How: Help the children trim their photos, removing most of the background. Have them glue the trimmed photos to cardboard. Cover the mounted photos with adhesive-backed paper and trim away the cardboard close to each picture. Help the children staple their mounted pictures to craft sticks, making stick puppets. Let children and their puppets say the rhyme below. Write the rhyme on a chart, and use this for language activities.

> Oh, look at this! This puppet is me.
> It's cute and strong as it can be.
> We have lots of friends
> As you can see,
> And we dance together 1-2-3!
> *(Children dance with their puppets.)*

Variation:
Have the children and their puppets say the rhyme below:

> Oh, look at this! These puppets are us.
> They have fun together; they never fuss.
> They dance together, round and round,
> Way up high, then near the ground.
> They have lots of friends
> As you can see,
> And they dance together 1-2-3.

This activity helps children learn about:
using rhyming sounds and working together with others.

All About Today
A Quick Trick with Photos

Gather These Materials:
photos of the children taken on the same day (see below)
plain paper, as many sheets as desired
construction paper, two sheets of any color
stapler and staples
marker

Where: anywhere at school

How: Gather the plain paper in a stack and place one sheet of construction paper on top of the stack and another on the bottom. Staple the stack along the left edge, making a blank book.

Take informal (not posed) photos of the children during one complete school day. Take at least one photo at each distinct part of your day: group time, center time, outdoor play time, snack preparation time, rest time, hand washing, and so on. Place the photos in chronological order in the book, and write a text that describes the day's activities. Use that day's date as the book's title. Be certain that each child is included in one or more of the pictures.

Variation:
Use your camera in this way to record a special event (making a scarecrow, planting a garden) from beginning to end. Make a book documenting the event.

This activity helps children learn about:
recording events and reading about them later.

Familiar Faces
A Quick Trick with Pictures of Familiar People

Gather These Materials:
paper copies of photos of familiar people
glue stick
cardboard
scissors (for adult use only)
clear, adhesive-backed paper

Where: anywhere to make the props
in the Block Area and Dramatic Play Area to play with the props

How: Take photos of familiar people—children in your group, others in the school, familiar school staff, parents, class visitors, the school's bus driver. Glue each picture to cardboard, cut around the figure, and laminate the figure with clear, adhesive-backed paper for stability. Place these "people" in the Block Area and encourage children to use them in their play.

Variation:
Place some of the "familiar faces" props in the Dramatic Play Area and some with construction toys such as table-size blocks. Encourage children to use these props in their play.

This activity helps children learn about:
vocabulary and language usage when making up roles for the props.

Funny Faces
A Quick Trick with Photos

Gather These Materials:
paper copies of photos of each child
lightweight cardboard
clear, adhesive-backed paper
scissors (for adult use only)

Where: anywhere to make the photos
on the floor or at a table to assemble the puzzles

How: Take a close-up photo of each child and make a large paper
copy of each photo. Glue each photo to lightweight cardboard
and cover with clear, adhesive-backed paper. Cut each photo
horizontally into three puzzle pieces with the eyes on one piece, the
nose on another and the mouth and chin on the third. Mix up all of
the puzzle pieces. Challenge children to put together the puzzle
pieces to make funny pictures out of familiar faces.

Variation:
Encourage the children to find puzzle pieces that go together to make
accurate pictures of children in the group.

This activity helps children learn about:
paying attention to details and about part/whole relationships.

Just for You, a Picture of Me
A Quick Trick with Craft Sticks

Gather These Materials:
photo of each child
craft sticks (four for each child)
glue
duct tape (cut in small pieces)
yarn
scissors (for adult use only)

Where: anywhere to take the photos
at a table to assemble the framed pictures

How: Take a photo of each child. The finished photo should fit into a frame the child will make from craft sticks. Cut the yarn into small pieces. Cut one for each child.

Have each child arrange four craft sticks in a square with the top and bottom sticks lying on top of the two side sticks. Have the child glue the sticks in place, forming a picture frame. Let the glue dry over night. Have the child glue the frame onto his photo, forming a framed photo. Help the children tape a loop of yarn to the top of their frames at the back. Children can give these framed photos as gifts to their families.

Variation:
Have the children make similar frames for photos of classroom activities. Designate a place to hang the photos, and use this area for a changing display of memorable moments caught by the camera.

This activity helps children learn about:
small motor coordination.

Matching My Friends
A Quick Trick with Children's Photos

Gather These Materials:
close-up photo of each child
index cards (twice as many cards as children)
glue stick
clear, adhesive-backed paper

Where: at a table to make the game
anywhere to play the game

How: Take a close-up photo of each child, and make two paper copies of each photo. (See p. 4 for instructions.) Copies should be the same size as the index cards or smaller.

Mount each copy on an index card. Cover all of the cards with clear, adhesive-backed paper for durability. If the cards curl, place them under heavy books for a few days to flatten them.

To play this game for two to four players, a child spreads out the photo cards, face down. In turn, a child turns up two cards. If the cards match, the child keeps the pair and takes another turn. If the cards don't match, the child turns them face down again. Children continue playing until all of the cards are matched. If desired, children can count their pairs to see who has the most matches.

Variation:
For a simpler game, incorporate a few "wild cards" into the deck. Draw a smiling face on an index card. Laminate to match the other cards. The game proceeds as above, but a wild card matches any other card that is turned. In this game, not all of the cards will be matched. Play continues until no matches are left.

This activity helps children learn about:
visual memory skills, counting and comparing.

My Name Looks Like This
A Quick Trick with Children's Photos

Gather These Materials:
scissors (for adult use only)
small paper copies of close-up photos of each child
glue stick
index cards (one per child)
fine-line marker
clear, adhesive-backed paper

Where: at a table to assemble the name cards

How: Trim each photo to fit onto part of an index card. Glue a child's picture to the upper left-hand corner of an index card. Write the child's name on the card and cover the card with clear, adhesive-backed paper for durability. Place the name cards in the Writing Area. Children can then copy their own and each other's names. Make an extra set of cards for the Art Area for children to copy when they need to write their names on their artwork.

Variation:
Use similar cards to label children's cubbies.

This activity helps children learn about:
recognizing their own and other children's written names.

Numbers of Interest
A Quick Trick with a Bulletin Board

Gather These Materials:
large, individual numerals (on paper or poster board)
bulletin board
any photos taken at school

Where: anywhere

How: Select familiar numerals that your children can read and understand. (At the beginning of the year, these may be numerals 1 to 5.) Hang the numerals in an interesting arrangement on a bulletin board. By each numeral, place the matching number of photos. Encourage the children to look at the photos and discuss what they see.

Variation:
Make a bulletin board using pictures of multiple people or items. Place pictures of one person or one item by the number 1; place pictures of two items or two people by the number 2, and so on.

This activity helps children learn about:
the relationship between numerals and counting.

Traveling Album
A Quick Trick with a Photo Album

Gather These Materials:
pictures of the children
photo album

Where: in class to initiate the project
in children's homes

How: Take informal pictures of the children engaged in their everyday activities. Include pictures of the group during movement activities, children and their structures in the Block Area, other center activities, cooking projects, art in progress, and outdoor play time. Also take pictures when you have classroom visitors and during field trips.

Place these photos in an album. Have a different child take the album home each night to share with families. Before the pictures go home, share them with the group and encourage the children to talk about each one. Don't put captions on the photos in the album. Encourage the children to talk with their families about the photos and the people in them.

Variation:
Keep a checklist of children's names and the number of photos they are in. You'll want to be sure that each child is included in several photos over a period of time.

This activity helps children learn about:
communicating with others about what happens in their day.

Quick Tricks for Learning ©2001 Monday Morning Books, Inc.

Doll Bed
A Quick Trick with a Cardboard Carton

Gather These Materials:
empty, heavy cardboard carton from copy paper (or similar carton)
craft knife (for adult use only)
wood-grained, adhesive-backed paper
patterned, adhesive-backed paper
small pillow
small baby blanket

Where: anywhere

How: Remove the top part of the carton by cutting all around the carton horizontally about 6 inches (15 cm) from the bottom. Discard the top. The bottom portion becomes a doll's bed that is 6 inches (15 cm) deep.

Cover the bed's outside with wood-grained, adhesive-backed paper and the inside with patterned, adhesive-backed paper. Put the small pillow inside for a mattress and add a small blanket. Make the bed available to the children for their dramatic play.

Variation:
Cut several cartons to bed size and let children turn them into beds for a hospital or other dramatic play scenes that require several beds.

This activity helps children learn about:
enhancing their play with simple props.

Washing Machine
A Quick Trick with a Cardboard Carton

Gather These Materials:
large, empty appliance-sized cardboard carton
strapping tape
craft knife (for adult use only)
hot glue gun
knob for a cabinet door or drawer
black permanent marker (for adult use only)

Where: anywhere

How: To make a washing machine from a cardboard carton, tape all flaps on the carton closed. The carton becomes the washing machine. To make a door for inserting and removing laundry, use the craft knife to make three straight cuts forming an upside-down U- shaped flap in one side of the carton. (This washing machine loads from the front, not the top.) The U-shaped flap becomes the washing machine's door. Glue the knob onto the door for easy opening and closing. Use the black marker to draw "on" and "off" and "hot" and "cold" controls on the washer.

Variation:
Make a refrigerator in a similar way using a tall, narrow carton.

This activity helps children learn about:
language development when they talk together during dramatic play.

Quick Tricks for Learning ©2001 Monday Morning Books, Inc.

Child-Size Table
A Quick Trick with a Cardboard Box

Gather These Materials:
heavy, cardboard box or carton (any size that suits you)
craft knife (for adult use only)
strapping tape
wood-patterned, adhesive-backed paper

Where: anywhere

How: Cut away or remove the box's top and discard. Turn the box upside-down, and use a craft knife to cut U shapes from each side. When you remove and discard these shapes, the remaining box parts become a table with legs. Apply strapping tape to the under side of the table to strengthen it. Turn the table right side up and cover it with wood patterned adhesive-backed paper. This little table is a perfect size for dolls, stuffed animals, and small children. (Boxes used for packing and transporting bottles are usually sturdy choices.)

Variation:
Paint the box with latex paint. If desired, use a light color, and invite the children to decorate the table with markers.

This activity helps children learn about:
language development when they talk together during dramatic play.

A House for Small Children
A Quick Trick with a Cardboard Carton

Gather These Materials:
large, empty cardboard carton
craft knife (for adult use only)
tempera paints and paint brushes
carpet samples, wallpaper samples, and glue (optional)

Where: anywhere you have room, indoors or outdoors

How: Use a large carton from an appliance or furniture store. Turn the box so that it is tall enough for children to stand inside. Cut a large flap in the side for a door, and cut a few windows. Tell the children that this will be their house. They'll enjoy painting their house, inside and out. If desired, give them carpet samples to place inside, and offer wallpaper samples and glue for the inside walls. Encourage the children to hang their artwork on the walls.

Variation:
Provide many appliance cartons over time, and have the children build a town or neighborhood with them.

This activity helps children learn about:
creative thinking and spatial concepts.

Quick Tricks for Learning ©2001 Monday Morning Books, Inc.

Sunny Faces
A Quick Trick with Peach Halves

Gather These Materials:
small, unbreakable dishes (one for each child)
serving spoons
canned peach halves (one for each child)
spoons (one for each child)
cottage cheese
raisins

Where: at a table

How: Have each child spoon a peach half into his own bowl with the cup side up. Have the children put a spoonful of cottage cheese into the peach's cup. Encourage them to use raisins to make facial features on the cottage cheese center. Then have them eat the "sunny faces." These sweet creations can be a snack, a dessert, or part of a meal.

Variation:
Do a similar activity using canned pear halves in place of the peaches.

This activity helps children learn about:
transferring food from one container to another.

Punchy Treat
A Quick Trick with Juices

Gather These Materials:
apple juice
cranberry juice
lemon-lime carbonated beverage
3 small plastic pitchers with handles and spouts
small paper cups (one for each child)
spoons for stirring

Where: at a table

How: As each child comes to make this treat, pour a small amount of apple juice into one pitcher, a small amount of cranberry juice into another, and a small amount of lemon-lime carbonated beverage into the third. Have each child pour the contents of all three pitchers into a paper cup, adding the carbonated beverage last. Tell the children to gently stir their concoctions and then enjoy the new taste sensation.

Variation:
Use any combination of fruit juices. Omit the lemon-lime beverage if desired.

This activity helps children learn about:
hand-eye coordination and preparing a snack.

Quick Tricks for Learning ©2001 Monday Morning Books, Inc.

Pumpkin Chiffon Pudding, 1-2-3
A Quick Trick with Cooked Pumpkin

Gather These Materials:
small paper bowls (one for each child)
measuring spoons
sugar
cooked pumpkin
undiluted, canned evaporated milk
cinnamon
prepared whipped topping
teaspoons (one for each child)
a freezer
marker

Where: at a table

How: Give each child a small bowl. Have each child mix together:
1 tablespoon sugar
2 tablespoons cooked pumpkin
3 tablespoons undiluted, canned evaporated milk
pinch cinnamon

Have the child stir in:
1 heaping tablespoon prepared whipped topping

Label the bowls with the children's names. Then place the bowls in the freezer for 45 minutes. Eat and enjoy!

Variation:
This recipe can be prepared in paper cups instead of a bowls.

This activity also helps children learn about:
how food tastes change when you combine them with other foods and spices.

Creamy Celery Boats
A Quick Trick with Celery

Gather These Materials:
washed celery stalks
knife (for adult use only)
small paper plates (one for each child)
finely chopped dried dates
whipped cream cheese
spoons or clean craft sticks for mixing- one for each child

Where: at a table

How: Cut the celery into pieces the size of your little finger. Give each child several pieces of celery and a few pieces of chopped dates. Place a small amount of whipped cream cheese on each child's plate. Have the children mix the dates into the cream cheese. Have them put a bit of the fruity spread in the "cup" of each of their celery pieces.

Variation:
Substitute drained crushed pineapple for the dates.

This activity helps children learn about:
preparing foods and trying new tastes.

Quick Tricks for Learning ©2001 Monday Morning Books, Inc.

My Favorite Squash
A Quick Trick with Squash

Gather These Materials:
a variety of squash including small, ripe zucchini and summer squash
salad dressing
sharp knife (for adult use only)
paper bowls (one per child)
a graph on large paper
glue stick
construction paper squash shapes for the graph
crayons or markers

Where: anywhere for children to explore the whole squash
at a table for eating the squash
around the graph for the graphing activity

How: Have the children explore a variety of whole squash. Help them to compare weights, textures, sizes, and shapes. Then cut the zucchini and summer squash into thin spears.

Serve the squash spears for a snack, giving one of each kind of squash to each child. Put a small amount of salad dressing in each bowl for the children to use for dipping. Let the children know which squash they are tasting, and encourage the children to talk about the differences and similarities in taste and texture.

Glue a picture of each sampled squash at the top of a two-column graph, gluing one picture above each column. Have each child write his name on a construction paper squash shape and glue that shape into the column that indicates which squash he liked best. Use the graph for comparison activities of more, less, more than, and less than.

Variation:
Repeat the activity with cooked squash.

This activity helps children learn about:
tasting new foods.

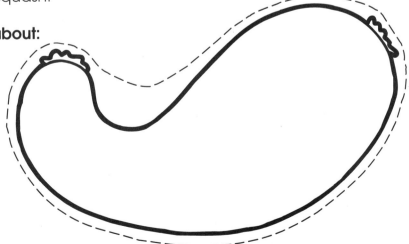

See-Through-the-Cover Book
A Quick Trick with a Plastic Report Cover

Gather These Materials:
colored construction paper (8 to 10 sheets)
plastic, see-through report cover (available at office supply stores)
slide-on plastic strip for binding the cover
marker

Where: at a table

How: Gather the construction paper pages in a stack. Remove the plastic, slide-on strip from the left side of the report cover. Open the plastic report cover with the folded side at your left, and slide the pages into place. Close the cover and slide the plastic strip over the folded side of the report cover. This forms a book with a see-through cover. Label each sheet of construction paper with its color name to create a concept book about colors.

Variation:
Show the children how to use this method to transform any pages they create into self-made books.

This activity helps children learn about:
recognizing color names and how to make their own books.

My Favorite Color
A Quick Trick with Photos

Gather These Materials:
construction paper in a variety of colors
camera

Where: anywhere

How: Have children tell you their favorite colors. Take an individual photo of each child holding a sheet of construction paper that is her favorite color. Use the photos to make a book titled "Our Favorite Colors." On each page, write the child's name and favorite color in this sentence:
"____'s favorite color is ____." Read the book to the group, then page through the book again while the group "reads" the pages with you. Place the book in the class library for children to read at will.

Variation:
Make large number cards with a different number on each card. Photograph the children holding their favorite numbers. With the photos, make a book similar to the one above.

This activity helps children learn about:
reading color and number names.

Alphabet Book
A Quick Trick with a Camera

Gather These Materials:
26 items, one for each consonant and short vowel sound
table and solid-colored tablecloth
letter cards
camera and accessories
three-hole punch
report cover with brads for three-hole paper
marker

How: Have the children help you gather an item for each letter of the alphabet. (Do this over a period of many days, gathering no more than five items on any given day. You might find pictures of items that begin with letters such as "q" and "x.")

Place one of the gathered items on the cloth-covered table. Beside it place the letter card that matches the item's beginning letter. Let a child help you take a picture of the item. Continue in this manner with the remaining items.

Process and make paper copies of all of the photos. Punch three holes in the left edge of every page. Place the photos in alphabetical order and bind them into the report cover. Write "Our ABC Book" on the cover. Read the book to the children, and then put it in the class library for them to read to each other.

Variation:
Use wallpaper from a sample book as the book cover. Use paper fasteners to hold the book together.

This activity helps children learn about:
alphabetical order and the relationship between letters and sounds.

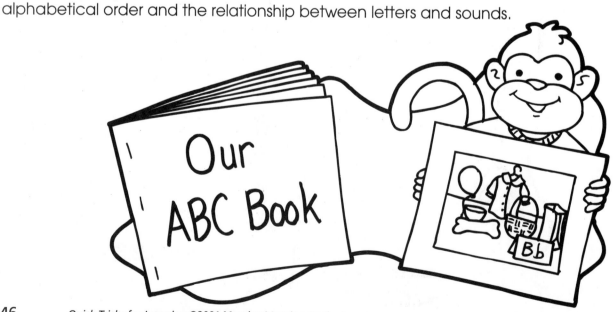

Counting In Our Room
A Quick Trick with a Plastic Report Cover

Gather These Materials:
common items found in the classroom
solid-colored table cloth (optional)
digital camera and accessories
plain paper
three-hole punch
report cover with brads for three-hole paper

Where: in the classroom

How: Tell the children that together you will make a counting book using the camera to take pictures of items in the room. In pairs, have the children gather common items from around the room. Have one pair bring one of an item; have another pair bring two of a different item; have others bring additional items from three to ten (examples: one puzzle, two chairs, three puppets, four crayons, five glue bottles, six blocks, seven trucks). Work with a few pairs of children in one day. Have each pair of children arrange their collection on a cloth-covered table or against a plain background on the floor.

Supervise as children take pictures of the items. Print out the pictures on separate sheets of plain paper, punch holes in each page, and then bind them in numeric order in a report cover.

Variation:
Make separate pictures of one child, two children, three children, and so on. Use the printed pictures to make a counting book.

This activity helps children learn about:
paying attention to details on book pages.

My Friends
A Quick Trick with Children's Photos

Gather These Materials:
photos of each of the children
photo album or blank book

Where: anywhere to prepare the album
at home to share the pictures with families

How: At the beginning of the year, take a picture of each child individually or of two or three children together. Be certain that each child is included only one time in the total collection of pictures. Place these photos in an album or a blank book labeled with the children's names. Let the children, in turn, take home the book to share with their families. This lets parents see and hear about their children's friends.

When the album is at school, place it in the class library so children can look through the pictures at will.

Variation:
Make copies of the pictures and make several books. (For instructions about making inexpensive paper copies, see p. 4.) Children won't have to wait so long before taking home the book.

This activity helps children learn about:
communicating with their families about their friends at school.

Familiar Places
A Quick Trick with Pictures of Familiar Places

Gather These Materials:
paper copies of photos of familiar places
2 sheets of construction paper
stapler and staples

Where: anywhere to make the props
Block Area and Dramatic Play Area to play with props

How: Take photos of familiar places—local family-style restaurants, a museum the group has visited, grocery stores, inside of a pediatrician's office, children's section of the library, fast-food restaurants, gasoline station, or school entrance, for example. Make same-size paper copies of each of these photos. Stack the papers between two sheets of construction paper, and then staple the pages along the left edge, forming a book.

Use the book with a small group of children. Have them look at one of the pictures and tell what the picture depicts. Encourage them to tell real or make-believe stories about the place in the picture. Repeat with other pictures.

Variation:
Use a puppet as a prop. Show the small group of children a picture in the book. Have the children make up a story about the puppet in the setting shown in the picture.

This activity helps children learn about:
vocabulary and language usage when they talk about the pictures.

Where's Teddy?
A Quick Trick with a Stuffed Animal

Gather These Materials:
stuffed animal
unit blocks
camera
marker
blank book

Where: in the Block Area

How: Select a stuffed animal. Have several children build a simple structure in the Block Area. Talk about words indicating position, such as *beside, inside, outside, over, under, near, far.* Let a few children place the stuffed animal in an interesting pose that illustrates the word "beside." Let one child use the camera to take a picture of the animal. Continue with other small groups and other place words. Place the photos in a blank book titled "Where's Teddy?" (Substitute the name of your animal.) Write an appropriate caption on each page, making a predictable book: "Teddy is <u>beside</u> the house." "Teddy is <u>on top of</u> the house."

Read the completed book to the children. Then place the book where it is available for them to look at when they desire. Send the book home with a different child each night. Children can "read" the book to their families.

Variation:
Do a similar activity outdoors. Captions might resemble these: "Teddy is <u>under</u> the tree." "Teddy is <u>inside</u> the sand box." "Teddy is <u>near</u> the slide." "Teddy is <u>far</u> from the swings."

This activity helps children learn about:
representing and using prepositions.

Space Ships Number Book
A Quick Trick with Space Ship Stickers

Gather These Materials:
4 sheets of plain paper
1 sheet of construction paper
marker
space ship stickers

Where: anywhere

How: Make a blank book by stacking the plain paper on top of the construction paper, folding the stack of papers in half horizontally, and stapling along the fold. Label the book "Space Ships". On the first page, stick one space ship sticker and write "One space ship is flying in outer space." On the second page, stick two space ship stickers and write "Two space ships are flying in outer space." Continue in this manner until the last page. On the final page, write "The End."

Variation:
Make a similar book using flower stickers. On the first page, write "One flower is growing in my garden." On the second page, write "Two flowers are growing in my garden." Continue as above.

This activity helps children learn about:
reading number names and seeing how singular and plural nouns use singular and plural verbs.

A Book of Sports Balls
A Quick Trick with Stickers

Gather These Materials:
4 sheets of plain paper
1 sheet of construction paper
marker
stickers that depict sports balls (baseball, soccer ball, football)

Where: anywhere

How: Make a blank book by stacking the plain paper on top of the construction paper, folding the stack of papers in half horizontally, and stapling along the fold. Label the book "Sports Balls." Stick two different sports balls on each page and label each page, for example, "One soccer ball and one football" or "One tennis ball and one basketball." Continue in this manner until you reach the last page. On the final page, write "The End."

Variation:
Make additional books putting three different stickers of sports balls on each page and labeling each page.

This activity helps children learn about:
using and reading the word "and."

one tennis ball and
one basketball

Our Library
A Quick Trick with a Cardboard Carton

Gather These Materials:
large empty cardboard carton
craft knife (for adult use only)
markers or tempera paints and paintbrushes
plain paper and index cards

Where: anywhere you have room

How: Use a large carton from an appliance or furniture store. Cut a door and a small window in the carton. Tell the children this carton will be a library, and invite them to decorate the box. They may draw bricks on the outside and books on the inside, or they might have other ideas. Let them decide what should be inside the library. Let the children take books inside for a "librarian" to "check out" and "check in." Provide paper so they can make signs and index cards to use as book cards. Encourage any ideas and efforts.

Allow the children to take dolls and stuffed animals inside to be their audience for a child-conducted Story Time. Following a field trip to the library is a good time to introduce this activity.

Variation:
Ask the children if they would like to gather their books in categories like the real library does. They could put books in categories such as fiction, nonfiction, animal books, books about tools, books about transportation, and song books.

This activity helps children learn about:
organizational skills, sorting by category, reading independently, reading with others, and reading to others.

Who Am I?
A Quick Trick with Portraits

Gather These Materials:
reproductions of art portraits (postcards, pictures in art books, posters)

Where: anywhere

How: Show the children a picture of a painted portrait that shows a full or partial figure. Have the children imitate the same pose in the portrait. In turn, have each child speak as though he is the painting's character. He might talk about what he is doing or about to do. He might tell why he is dressed in a particular way. Ask the children open-ended questions that allow them to explain more about themselves as the imagined person.

Over a period of time, show children a variety of portraits, both formal and casual, of people of different cultures. Show pictures that contain more than one person. Encourage the children to use their imaginations to discuss who the people are and what they are doing.

Variation:
Have a child strike a pose in front of the group. Have the children draw a stick figure picture of the child in that pose.

This activity helps children learn about:
using a picture to spark imaginative story telling.

Where Am I?
A Quick Trick With Landscapes and Seascapes

Gather These Materials:
reproductions of landscapes and seascapes, city scenes and rural scenes (postcards, note cards, pictures in art books from the library)

Where: anywhere

How: Show the children a picture of a landscape (or other scene), and ask them to describe what they see. What location do they think the painting shows (city, farm, lake)? Have them describe the weather. What clues help them make their decision (sun, clouds, trees leaning in the wind)? Ask the children to use their imaginations to think about what might have happened at the setting a few minutes before. What do they think will happen there a few minutes later? Tonight? Tomorrow?

Variation:
Look for children's picture books with detailed pictures. Choose a book the children might not be familiar with, and show them a picture from the book. Have them talk about the story the picture tells. Then read the book to the children.

This activity helps children learn about:
Paying attention to detail.

What's Happening Here?
A Quick Trick with Still Life Pictures

Gather These Materials:
reproductions of still life art (postcards, posters, pictures in art books)

Where: anywhere

How: Show the children a picture of a still life painting and ask them to describe what they see. Why do they think those items are gathered together? Who might have put them there? What do the children think happened there a few minutes before? What do they think might happen there tomorrow? Encourage all answers.

Variation:
Challenge the children to place classroom items into a "still life" arrangement. They can make arrangements in the Art Area, the Dramatic Play Area, or other classroom areas. Encourage them to use natural materials outdoors to create still life arrangements.

This activity helps children learn about:
using their imaginations.

Art Is All Around
A Quick Trick with Framed Art

Gather These Materials:
framed art

Where: in the classroom

How: Some libraries have framed art to lend for a period of time. Check out framed art and hang it in your classroom. Discuss the paintings with the children. Help them learn the names of the paintings and the artists. Change the artwork each month.

   (If your library doesn't offer this service, use inexpensive frames to frame calendar pictures or posters or postcards of fine art.)

Variation:
Encourage the children to talk about the colors and shapes in the pictures. Make art materials available so they can create their own pictures using similar colors and shapes.

This activity helps children learn about:
the variety of art styles.

Game Spinner
A Quick Trick with Cardboard and a Paper Clip

Gather These Materials:
scissors (for adult use only)
poster board
marker
clear, adhesive-backed paper
sharp pointed object for punching a hole
vinyl-clad paper clip
brass paper fastener
strapping tape

Where: at a table

How: Cut a 5-inch (12.5 cm) circle from poster board. With a marker, divide the circle horizontally and vertically to form four equal parts. Program the spinner as needed for your game. (For example, write a different numeral in each section, or write "directions," such as "+1," "-1," "+2," "-2.")

Cover the circle with clear, adhesive-backed paper for durability. Punch a hole in the center of the circle. Cut a 1/2-inch (1.25 cm) square piece of poster board and punch a hole in its center. Make a stack with the large circle on the bottom, then the small square (with its hole directly over the hole on the larger piece), then the paper clip. Slide the paper fastener through the smallest opening of the paper clip and through the two poster board holes. Open the fastener's prongs at the bottom of the stack, being sure that the fastener isn't too tight. (The paper clip must be able to spin.) Secure the prongs with several pieces of masking tape. Flick the paper clip with the snap of a finger to make the clip spin. The clip, when it stops, indicates the next move in a game.

Variation:
The spinner can be divided into more parts for more spinning options.

This activity helps children learn about:
following directions when children use the spinner as part of a game.

Sticky Numbers
A Quick Trick with Sticky Notes

Gather These Materials:
fine-tip marker
10 "sticky" notes
marker
ruler
strip of poster board
clear, adhesive-backed paper

Where: anywhere

How: Use the fine-tip marker to number the "sticky" notes from 1 to 10. With the ruler and the standard marker, divide the strip of poster board into 10 sections. Number the sections in order from 1 to 10, starting at the left. Cover the strip with clear, adhesive-backed paper for durability.

In a small group, distribute the "sticky" note numerals to the children. Have children place their numbered notes in the correct grid spaces. Give clues, when necessary, for example, "It's between six and eight." When the numbers are all placed, remove and redistribute the notes, then play again. Later, place the game where children can play with it at will.

Variation:
As the children's familiarity with numbers increases, make new game boards and new "sticky" notes, adding numbers ten at a time (teens, twenties, thirties, and so on).

This activity helps children learn about:
ordering numbers.

Apples and Apple Seeds
A Quick Trick with Apple Seeds

Gather These Materials:
apple patterns (p. 61)
55 apple seeds
paper towels
red poster board
scissors (for adult use only)

Where: anywhere

How: Use the template to cut eleven apple shapes from the red poster board. Collect apple seeds when children are eating apple snacks. When you have 55 seeds, wash them and put them on paper towels to dry. (If desired, instead of apple seeds use small dried, black beans.)

      With a marker, number the apple shapes from 0 to 10. Show children how to spread out the apples and put the correct number of seeds on each apple shape.

Variation:
Encourage the children to place the apples in order from 0 to 10.

This activity helps children learn about:
counting and seriation.

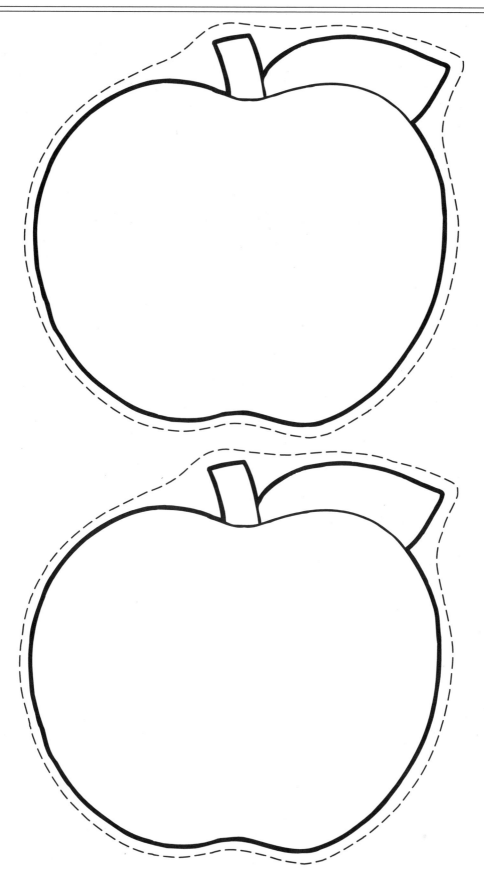

Feed the Elephants
A Quick Trick with Peanuts

Gather These Materials:
elephant patterns (p. 63)
permanent, fine-line marker
tape or glue
scissors (for adult use only)
4 berry baskets
4-inch (10 cm) lengths of yarn
one wooden cube
bags of peanuts roasted in the shell
large basket/box to contain all of the game pieces

Where: at a table to construct the game
anywhere to play the game

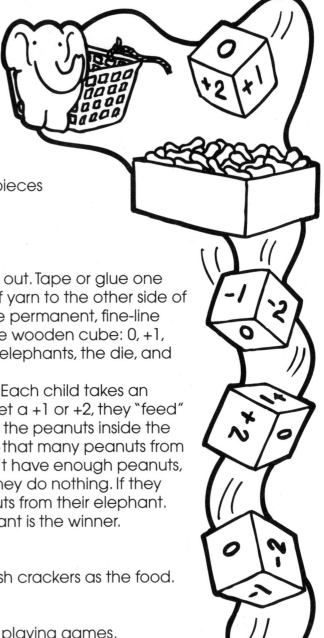

How: Duplicate four elephants and cut them out. Tape or glue one elephant to each berry basket. Tie a length of yarn to the other side of the basket for the tail. To make the die, use the permanent, fine-line maker to write the following on the sides of the wooden cube: 0, +1, +2, -1, -2, a sad face. Gather the berry basket elephants, the die, and the peanuts in a large basket or box.

   Up to four children can play this game. Each child takes an elephant. In turn, children roll the die. If they get a +1 or +2, they "feed" their elephant that many peanuts (by putting the peanuts inside the berry basket). If they get -1 or -2, they remove that many peanuts from their elephant (berry basket), unless they don't have enough peanuts, in which case they do nothing. If they get 0, they do nothing. If they get a sad face, they remove all of their peanuts from their elephant. The first child to have 10 peanuts in her elephant is the winner.

Variation:
Create turtles from margarine tubs. Use goldfish crackers as the food.

This activity helps children learn about:
taking turns and other social skills required for playing games.

Note:
Check to see if any of the children have peanut allergies.

Quick Tricks for Learning ©2001 Monday Morning Books, Inc.

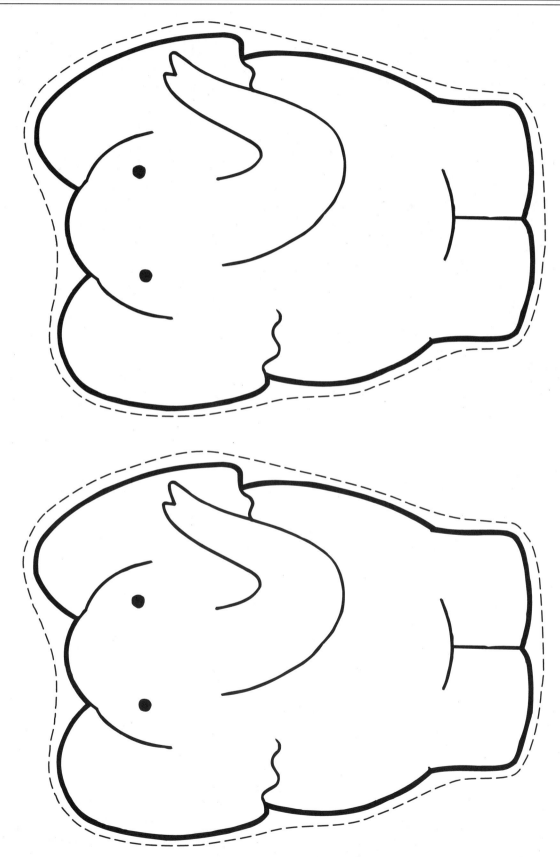

Concentrate On This
A Quick Trick with Blocks and Deli Containers

Gather These Materials:
A variety of pairs of blocks
12 identical, opaque deli food containers

Where: on the floor or at a table

How: With a small group of children, gather six pairs of different colored blocks (two red blocks, two green blocks, two blue blocks, and so on). Separate and mix up the blocks, and then spread them on a surface in front of the small group. Cover each block with an inverted, opaque deli food container. Slide the items around on the surface to make sure they are mixed up.

To play the game, each child takes a turn removing two food containers revealing the block beneath each. If the blocks match, the child keeps the blocks and moves the empty deli containers out of the way. If the blocks don't match, the child covers them again with the deli containers. The next child takes a turn, and play continues until all of the blocks have been uncovered. Have children return their blocks to the center of the playing area, cover them with deli containers, and begin the game again. Make the game more challenging by adding more pairs of blocks.

Variation:
If you do not have blocks, use pairs of colored paper wads created from six different colors of paper scraps.

This activity helps children learn about:
increasing memory skills.

Five Little Ducks
A Quick Trick with a File Folder

Gather These Materials:
duckling patterns (p. 66)
heavy paper
markers (including red)
file folder
scissors (for adult use only)
glue
envelope

Where: at a table to prepare the game
anywhere to play the game

How: Duplicate the five ducklings onto heavy paper and cut them out. Draw one Mama duck on the inside of the file folder. Print the rhyme (below) opposite Mama duck. Write the numerals in red. Glue an envelope to the back of the file folder to hold the ducklings.

   After the children have learned the rhyme during Large Group Time, show them the folder. Have them say the rhyme while one child (or the adult) "follows along," using the ducklings to "act out" the rhyme. Make the folder and ducks available for the children to play with at will.

> Five Little Ducks
> (adapted traditional)
> FIVE little ducks went out one day
> Over the hills and far away. *(Move 5 ducks away from Mother.)*
> Mother duck called, "Quack, quack, quack, quack."
> But only FOUR little ducks came back.
> *(Remove one duck; move 4 ducks back to their mother and count these remaining ducks with the children.)*
> FOUR little ducks went out one day
> *(Repeat until NO ducks come back.)*
> Sad mother duck looked out one day
> Over the hills and far away.
> Mother duck cried, "QUACK, QUACK, QUACK QUACK!" *(Cry loudly.)*
> And all of her five little ducks came back.
> *(Put the five ducklings near the Mama.)*

Variation:
Let the children act out this rhyme themselves.

This activity helps children learn about:
subtracting by one and rhyming sounds.

Duckling Patterns

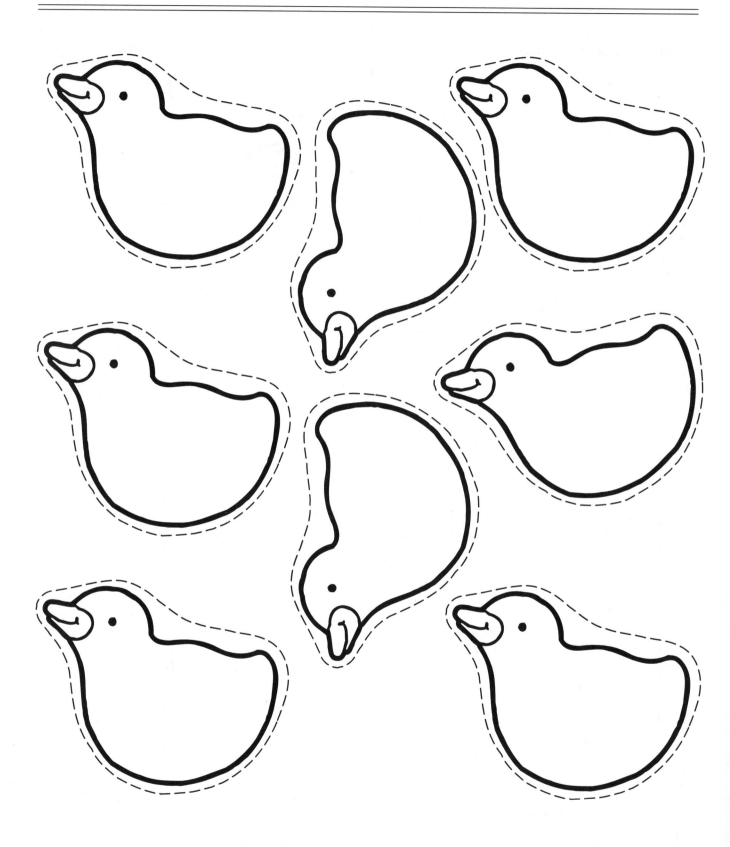

Quick Tricks for Learning ©2001 Monday Morning Books, Inc.

Gingerbread Sizes
A Quick Trick with Gingerbread Figures

Gather These Materials:
scissors (for adult use only)
brown poster board
manila envelope
clear, adhesive-backed paper
markers

Where: at a table to make the game
anywhere to play the game

How: On the poster board, draw, then cut out, five gingerbread figures of greatly different sizes. The largest should fit easily into the manila envelope. Decorate the figures as desired. Laminate the figures by covering them with clear, adhesive-backed paper. Draw a gingerbread figure on the envelope's front, and label the envelope "Gingerbread Sizes." Put the figures in the envelope.

　　To play the game, a child takes the figures out of the envelope, mixes them up, and then arranges them in order by size from largest to smallest or from smallest to largest.

Variation:
As the children's skill increases, add more figures to the game.

This activity helps children learn about:
seriation.

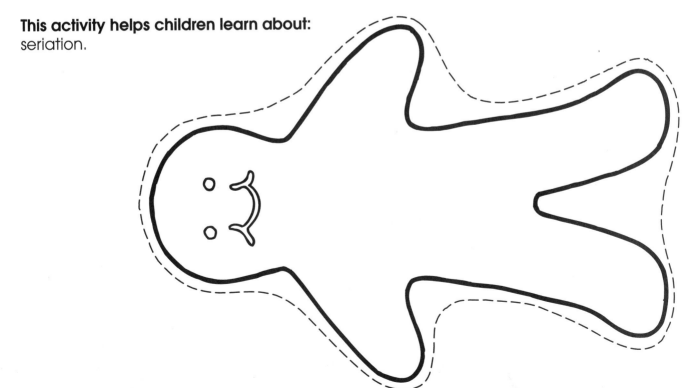

Gingerbread Buttons
A Quick Trick with Buttons

Gather These Materials:
marker
brown poster board
scissors (for adult use only)
clear, adhesive-backed paper or laminating film
35 small buttons
plastic zipper bag

Where: at a table to make the game
anywhere to play the game

How: Draw 10 gingerbread figures on the poster board. Cut out the figures. Draw vests on the figures. On each vest, write a numeral, 0 to 9. Laminate the figures and store them with the buttons in a plastic zipper bag.

　　To play the game, the child spreads out the gingerbread figures and puts the correct number of buttons on each figure's vest. When she has finished matching the gingerbread figures and their buttons, she asks a friend to check her work, giving another child practice with number/numeral relationships.

Variation:
Encourage the children to put the gingerbread figures in numerical order from left to right.

This activity helps children learn about:
counting out real objects to match the correct numeral.

Goin' Fishin'
A Quick Trick with Clothespins

Gather These Materials:
10 pieces of yarn cut in 14-inch (35-cm) lengths
10 wooden, spring-type clothespins
glue gun (for adult use only)
scissors (for adult use only)
poster board
markers
plastic zipper bag

Where: on the floor

How: Tie a clothespin onto the end of each piece of yarn. Secure the yarn with a dab of glue from the glue gun. Write a different numeral (0 to 9) on each clothespin. From poster board, cut 10 fish shapes. On each shape, draw a number of dots corresponding to the numbers on the clothespins. Leave one fish blank (to match the number zero). Place all items in a plastic zipper bag.

   To use the activity, a child lines up the fishing lines and hooks (clothespins) on the floor. She looks at the numeral on a clothespin, finds the fish with the matching number of dots, and then clips the fish to the clothespin. When she has caught all of the fish, she throws them all back (unclips them) and returns the components to the zipper bag, ready for the next player.

Variation:
Make a similar matching game with letters and pictures of items that begin with the consonant sound represented by each letter.

This activity helps children learn about:
matching amounts with the numerals that represent them.

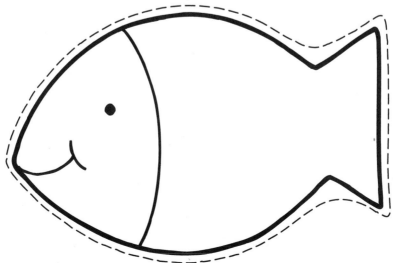

Hungry Caterpillar Counting Game
A Quick Trick with Snack Foods

Gather These Materials:
The Very Hungry Caterpillar by Eric Carle (Philomel, 1987)
waxed paper, one sheet for each child
bowls (one per each type of food)
small snack foods: cereals, raisins, small pretzels, dried fruit, and so on

Where: at a table

How: Read *The Very Hungry Caterpillar* by Eric Carle to the children. At snack time, give each child a sheet of waxed paper to use as a clean working surface. Encourage the children to line up on their waxed paper one cereal flake, two raisins, three banana chips, four pieces of dried apple, and so on. As a group, make up a story about hungry children who ate one cereal flake, two raisins, and so on. Have the children eat their snack items as they make up the story.

Variation:
Have children count their snack items into a paper cup as they make up the story. They can take these outdoors at playtime.

This activity helps children learn about:
seriation and counting for meaning.

... one cereal flake

I'm So Sorry
A Quick Trick with Picture Rhyming Cards

Gather These Materials:
cards depicting rhyming words (cat/hat), with one picture per card

Where: anywhere

How: Gather a group of three or more children. Any number can play as long as there are enough cards. Mix up the cards and place them face down in a deck. Have each child take two or three cards. Place the remaining cards (if any) in the middle of the group. If any children receive two rhyming cards during the deal, they return them to the center of the deck and draw again.

In turn, each child asks one other child in the group, "Do you have a picture that rhymes with <u>(says the name of one of his pictures)</u>?" The child who is called on looks at her cards. If she has a match, she says, "Yes, I do," and she gives the matching card to the first child who puts the matching cards together and sets them aside. The asking child draws another card from the pile as long as cards remain. Play passes to the next child.

If the child who is asked has no match, she says, "I'm so sorry." The requesting player's turn is over and the next child in the circle tries to locate a match. Play continues until all rhyming cards are matched.

Variations:
Play a similar game using alphabet cards with some cards in upper case and the matches in lower case.

This activity helps children learn about:
rhyming sounds, asking and answering politely, listening, paying attention, and taking turns.

Names and Faces
A Quick Trick with Index Cards

Gather These Materials:
pen or marker
index cards (one per child)
same-size photos of each child
basket or plastic zipper bag

Where: anywhere

How: Write a child's name on each index card. Place the cards and the photos in a basket or a plastic zipper bag. To play the game, children spread the photos on the floor and look through the index cards to find the matching name for each child. Children place the name cards on the matching photos. Encourage them to ask their friends to check and make sure the items match. (When others check the work, they too benefit from the activity.)

Variation:
Take pictures of familiar people at school—the cook, the custodian, the librarian—and make a similar game using their names and photos.

This activity helps children learn about:
decoding words.

Quick Tricks for Learning ©2001 Monday Morning Books, Inc.

Letters Into Words
A Quick Trick with Sentence Strips

Gather These Materials:
marker
sentence strips
scissors (for adult use only)
plastic zipper bag

Where: anywhere

How: On a sentence strip, print a word that pertains to a current area of the children's interest (circus, motorcycle, brontosaurus, farm). Now print the word again on another sentence strip, making two identical cards. Leave a bit of extra space between the letters on each strip. Cut apart the letters of one strip and put these and the other strip into a plastic zipper bag.

  To use the activity, children empty the contents and place the whole strip in front of themselves. They use the individual letters to form the word just below the whole word. Encourage them to read the word. Repeat this activity using other words of interest to the children. Bag each word and matching letters separately.

Variation:
Make a similar, individual activity for each child by writing the child's phone number on both strips. Cut one of the strips into individual numerals. Children will quickly learn their own phone numbers when they play with this activity.

This activity helps children learn about:
recognizing letters and numerals and matching visual shapes.

Alphabet Dance
A Quick Trick with the Alphabet

Gather These Materials:
thick-line, permanent marker
4 by 6-inch (10 by 15-cm) pieces of poster board, 26 pieces
clear, adhesive-backed paper for laminating
scissors (for adult use only)
CD or tape player with CDs or tapes

Where: at a table to make the game pieces
any open space to play the game

How: Use the marker to write one alphabet letter on each piece of poster board. Cover each card with clear, adhesive-backed paper and trim the clear paper to fit.

To play the game, spread the cards around the space in a path—a circle works well. Have each child stand beside a letter. Play the music, stopping it every 15 seconds or so. While the music plays, children follow each other around the path. When the music stops, children go to the nearest letter. In turn, five children tell the others the names of their letters. The music begins and the game continues. Be certain each child has several opportunities to identify letters. If a child does not know a letter's name, have the group identify the letter together. If the group does not know, identify the letter for them, then begin the game again.

Variation:
Make number cards (0 to 10), and use them in the same way. When children have learned to recognize numerals 0 to 10, add 11 to 19.

This activity helps children learn about:
large motor control, paying attention, following directions, and letter recognition.

Beach Ball Categories
A Quick Trick with a Beach Ball

Gather These Materials:
inflated beach ball

Where: in a space with no breakable objects

How: Have children sit in a circle. Select a category pertaining to things you have talked about in class: colors, numbers, letters, animal names, insects, or community helpers, for example. Toss the ball to one child, who names something in that category before tossing the ball to another child. Each child who catches the ball names an item before tossing the ball to another child. If the ball goes outside the circle, the child who retrieves it names an item before tossing the ball to restart the game. Do not be rigid about answers. Accept repeats of an earlier answer. If incorrect answers are given, correct gently.

Variation:
If you do not have a beach ball, use a lightweight plastic ball.

This activity helps children learn about:
large motor control, using language, and thinking and responding quickly.

Craft Stick Puzzles
A Quick Trick with Jumbo Craft Sticks

Gather These Materials:
jumbo craft sticks (or tongue depressors)
masking tape
pencil
cookie cutter with a simple shape
permanent marker
construction paper to match the marker's color
scissors (for adult use only)
glue stick
large index card
clear, adhesive-backed paper
plastic zipper bag

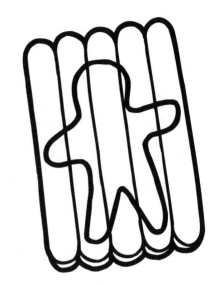

Where: at a table to make the puzzle
anywhere to play with the puzzle

How: Lay five or six jumbo craft sticks on the table with sides touching. Put a strip of tape across the top of the sticks and another across the bottom to hold the sticks in place, forming the puzzle's face. Place a cookie cutter in the center of the puzzle's face. With a pencil, trace around the cookie cutter. Color in the traced shape with permanent marker. Remove and discard the tape. Separate the sticks and mix them up. You now have a puzzle. Trace the same cookie cutter onto the paper and cut out the paper shape. Glue the shape to the index card and cover this with clear, adhesive-backed paper.

Children look at the index card picture and then arrange the sticks to reconstruct the puzzle. Store the puzzle and the picture in a plastic zipper bag. Make more puzzles of different colors and store them and their matching pictures in separate bags.

Variation:
Store two different puzzles in the same bag. This adds to the challenge.

This activity helps children learn about:
small motor control, visual discrimination, and problem-solving skills.

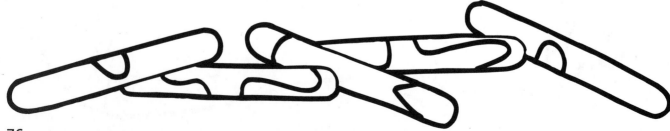

Quick Tricks for Learning ©2001 Monday Morning Books, Inc.

Do as I Do
A Quick Trick with a Magic Wand

Gather These Materials:
1 sheet of construction paper, any color
tape
scissors (for adult use only)
one 5-inch (12.5 cm) square of yellow construction paper

Where: anywhere

How: To make a magic wand, tightly roll the sheet of construction paper, yielding a thin tube. Wrap tape around the tube in several places to hold it tight. Cut a star from the yellow construction paper. Tape the star to one end, forming a magic wand.

For this circle game, choose a leader to stand in the center of the circle. The leader holds the magic wand. All children sing the song below, and the leader makes a motion (waving, jumping, hopping, stretching and swaying, or marching, for example).

> Tune: "Farmer In the Dell"
> I have the magic wand.
> I have the magic wand.
> Whatever I do,
> Please do it, too.
> I have the magic wand.
>
> I have the magic wand.
> I have the magic wand.
> When I am through
> I pass it to you. *(Child hands wand to another child.)*
> You have the magic wand.

The child who is given the wand moves into the circle to be the new leader. The child who chose him takes the other child's vacated space. The group begins singing, the new leader makes a motion, and the game continues.

Variation:
Cover the star on the wand with gold glitter.

This activity helps children learn about:
leading a group and paying attention.

Hop To the Square
A Quick Trick with Carpet Samples

Gather These Materials:
carpet samples in a variety of colors
large permanent marker
tape/CD player and tapes/compact discs (optional)

Where: in a large room or outdoors

How: Using a variety of shapes, draw one shape on each carpet sample. Make several carpets of each shape. Scatter the samples around the room. Ask a child to name a way of moving (walking backwards, crawling, hopping, or skipping, for example), and ask another child to name a shape. All children move in the way chosen and they move to a carpet that has the named shape. Continue playing until every child has had a turn to name a way of moving and a shape. Children will have opportunities for problem solving when they share rugs with several friends. For additional fun, add music to this activity and have children move in rhythm to the music.

Variation:
Use sidewalk chalk to draw shapes on the concrete surface of an empty parking lot and play the game there.

This activity helps children learn about:
problem solving and cooperation.

Quick Tricks for Learning ©2001 Monday Morning Books, Inc.

Let's Fly a Kite
A Quick Trick with a Paper Bag

Gather These Materials:
paper grocery bag (one per child)
tape
hole punch
36-inch (90 cm) lengths of yarn (one per child)
crepe paper streamers (optional)
stapler and staples (optional)
markers or stickers (optional)

Where: anywhere to make the kite
outdoors to fly the kite

How: To make a simple kite, fold back the top 3 inches (7.5 cm) of a grocery bag, and secure it with a few strips of tape. Punch one hole in each of two opposite sides of the bag's top. Thread the yarn through the two holes and tie the ends together, making a loop. This is the kite's "string." If desired, staple crepe paper streamers to the bottom corners of the bag, and decorate the bag with markers or stickers.
　　To fly the kite, have the child hold onto the yarn loop, hold out his arm, and run. Air will fill the bag, causing the kite to billow behind him.

Variation:
For a really quick trick, use shopping bags or gift bags as kites. Tie the handles together with the end of an 18-inch (45-cm) length of yarn. Have the child hold the yarn's other end as the kite string.

This activity helps children learn about:
following directions and recycling materials.

Move Like This
A Quick Trick with the Body

Gather These Materials:
none

Where: anywhere

How: Gather children in a group or in a circle. One child is the
leader. He names a body part and suggests a way to move it.
Children follow his lead while singing the song below. At the end
of the song, the leader chooses another leader. Play continues until
every child has been the leader.

> Tune: "Mary Had a Little Lamb"
>
> Move your fingers just like this,
> Just like this, just like this.
> Move your fingers just like this,
> Then clap and turn around.

Children may bend, tap, point, or move their
fingers in many other ways.

Variation:
Engage in a similar activity with children moving their whole bodies
(swaying, jumping, or hopping, for example). Change the words of
the song to reflect this difference:

> Move your body just like this,
> Just like this, just like this.
> Move your body just like this,
> Then clap and turn around.

This activity helps children learn about:
naming body parts, listening, watching, and following directions.

Quick Tricks for Learning ©2001 Monday Morning Books, Inc.

Move Your Streamers
A Quick Trick with Paper Streamers

Gather These Materials:
18-inch (45-cm) long crepe paper streamers (one or more per child)

Where: anywhere

How: Give each child one or more streamers. Children hold these and sing the following song, moving the streamers as the song suggests:

> Tune: "Here We Go Round the Mulberry Bush"
>
> Move your streamers round and round,
> Round and round, round and round,
> Move your streamers round and round,
> Round and round like this.
>
> Move your streamers up and down,
> Up and down, up and down,
> Move your streamers up and down,
> Up and down like this.

Sing other verses, substituting motions that the children suggest.

Variation:
Give children streamers of two colors, one for each hand. Use color names in the song. Children move only the streamers that are named:

> Move red streamers round and round,
> Round and round, round and round,
> Move red streamers round and round,
> Round and round like this.
>
> Move blue streamers up and down,
> Up and down, up and down,
> Move blue streamers up and down,
> Up and down like this.

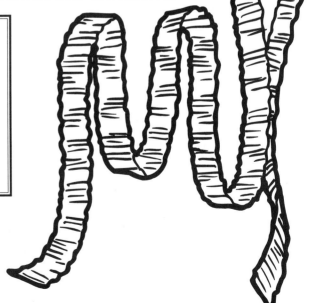

This activity helps children learn about:
listening, observing and imitating actions.

Sock It to Me
A Quick Trick with Discarded Socks

Gather These Materials:
clean, discarded athletic socks
large cardboard boxes
chalk

Where: in a large, open space, or outdoors

How: Roll one sock into a ball. Stuff the ball into the toe of another sock. Twist the second sock just above the ball, then fold back the second sock's top over the ball so the inside of the second sock's top is now on the outside. Twist the extra material, and then fold the edge over the top. You now have a sock ball. Make several of these so that a number of children can play at the same time.

Place cardboard boxes, open ends up, at random in a large, open area. Children throw the sock balls at the boxes, which are targets. At first children can throw from any distance or direction. As their throwing skill increases, encourage them to draw chalk lines, which they can stand behind while throwing the balls.

Draw a different shape on each box. Children tell which shape is on the target they hit. Substitute numerals or letters for shapes, if desired.

Variation:
For a more challenging activity, write numerals on each of the boxes. Children throw two sock balls at each turn and add the two numerals to tell their score.

This activity helps children learn about:
motor control and making toys from recycled materials.

Quick Tricks for Learning ©2001 Monday Morning Books, Inc.

Floating Clouds
A Quick Trick with a Bed Sheet

Gather These Materials:
a bed sheet (for a small group, use half of a twin sheet)

Where: outdoors or in a large, open area indoors

How: Have most of the children stand around the perimeter of a bed sheet and hold onto the edges before them. Several of the children should stand at the edge of the sheet without holding on. Children holding the sheet begin with the sheet at waist level. Have them do what the words describe, raising and lowering their arms. On the final two lines, the children who have not been holding onto the sheet, run under the sheet and cross to the other side before the sheet comes down. Substitute other movement words such as *crawl, hop, walk backwards,* or *gallop* for the underlined word.

Arms up high; cloud goes high.
Arms down low; cloud goes low.
Arms up high; cloud goes high.
Arms down low; cloud goes low.
Arms up high and friends <u>run</u> across
Arms down low. Don't be slow.

Variation:
For the final two lines, substitute the words below. Have some children run under the sheet and hide underneath as the sheet comes down.

Arms up high, friends run inside.
Arms down low. Where did they go?

This activity helps children learn about:
focusing attention, listening, and following directions.

Exploring Textures
A Quick Trick with Everyday Items

Gather These Materials:
sensory table (water table or sand table or see Variation)
a variety of everyday items such as sand, water, dried beans, or dirt
plastic containers (canisters, deli containers, bowls)

Where: at a sensory table

How: Put a few inches of water in the sensory table. Provide children with plastic containers filled with an item such as the ones listed above. Encourage the children to incorporate the new item into the water and to talk about how the item and the water change. (The item may become soggy; the water may change color or become cloudy; the water may feel thicker.) Have the children predict what will happen if they add more of the substance, then give them more of the item and let them check their predictions.

On other days, offer different items from the list or other items that are readily available. On some days, offer several different items to add. Repeat the activity, beginning with sand instead of water. Give the children water to add to the sand and ask them to predict how the added water will change the sand. Let them check their predictions. Offer a variety of items over a succession of days. Encourage the children to talk about the changes they observe.

Variation:
If you don't have a sensory table, use large, shallow plastic storage containers set on a table or on the ground.

This activity helps children learn about:
exploring with their senses and talking about their experiences.

Charming Bracelets
A Quick Trick with Pipe Cleaners

Gather These Materials:
pipe cleaners

Where: anywhere

How: In turn, show each child how to bend a pipe cleaner into a circle and then twist the ends together to hold it tight. As the child makes bracelets, have her put them on her arm. Each time she adds one, recite this rhyme, then have her count her bracelets:

> Bracelets, bracelets
> Have such charm.
> How many bracelets
> On my arm? 1, 2, 3, 4, and so on

Encourage the children to count each other's bracelets. When a child has more bracelets than she can count, have her move some bracelets to her other arm and then count the bracelets on each arm. When she again has too many to count, stop the counting game and just make bracelets for fun.

Variation:
Count just the blue bracelets, the yellow ones, and so on.

This activity helps children learn about:
counting and number combinations.

Human Graph
A Quick Trick with Clothes

Gather These Materials:
none

Where: in the room

How: Have half of the children stand before the remaining sitting group. Have those who are wearing a particular color, such as blue, stand in line. Count these children. Have children who are not wearing that color stand in another line. Count these children. Now have the lines stand side-by-side and have children in the shorter line each hold hands with one person in the longer line, forming a human bar graph. Discuss the numbers of people in each line. Which line is longer? Which is shorter? How many children do not have a partner? How many more children would the shorter line need to make each line the same?

Have the sitting and standing children trade places and repeat the activity.

At other times, compare other clothing traits using the children in a human graph. For instance, children in long sleeves and children in short sleeves; children with jackets and children without jackets; children wearing stripes and children not wearing stripes.

Variation:
After forming the human graph, use child-shaped (or gingerbread-shaped) precut shapes to represent the information on a paper graph.

This activity helps children learn about:
observing, counting, comparing, and graphing.

Nylon Balls
A Quick Trick with Pantyhose

Gather These Materials:
clean, discarded pantyhose (several pairs)

Where: anywhere

How: Cut the legs from several pairs of pantyhose. Crumple one leg into a ball and put it inside another leg, pushing the ball into the toe of the second leg. Twist the leg tightly just above the inserted ball, then push the ball against the twist, pushing the ball backwards into the leg. The leg will turn inside out. Push the ball as far as it will go, then twist the leg just above the ball. Continue in this manner until the entire leg is used up. Tie a knot at the open end of the leg. You now have a small, soft nylon ball. These balls are safe indoors, and because they are soft, they are great for children who are just learning how to catch. The balls are sturdy, so they can be washed in warm water in a washing machine.

Variation:
For larger balls, begin by crumpling together several pantyhose legs as the interior part of the ball.

This activity helps children learn about:
motor control, throwing, catching, and recycling familiar items.

Puppet Stories
A Quick Trick with Puppets

Gather These Materials:
chart
markers
a variety of puppets

Where: anywhere

How: Discuss story beginnings. Help the children think up imaginative openings for a variety of stories. Record the suggestions on a chart. Here are a few to get you started:

- "I walked into the room and saw a big box wrapped with shiny gold paper and tied with a big purple ribbon."
- "(Puppet's name) had never seen a swimming pool before."
- "One night, mother made something for dinner that smelled very strange."
- "Have you ever been to a restaurant that was just for animals? We have, and this is what it's like."
- "My neighbor got the strangest pet for his birthday."

Use commercially available puppets or have children make puppets using any materials and methods. Have children form groups of three. Read one of the story beginnings, and have a group use their puppets to act out a story based on that beginning. Their stories may be only a few sentences. Encourage all efforts. Continue the activity until every child has had an opportunity to participate.

Variation:
On another occasion, read the children the opening sentences from familiar books. Have them act out in small groups a story the opening inspires. Encourage all creative responses.

This activity helps children learn about:
creative thinking, taking turns, and cooperation.

Quick Tricks for Learning ©2001 Monday Morning Books, Inc.

Sorting by Size
A Quick Trick with a Favorite Story

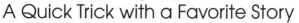

Gather These Materials:
cutout pictures of three different-sized snowpeople
glue stick
poster board
clear, adhesive-backed paper (optional)
3 bowls of greatly different sizes
3 spoons of greatly different sizes
3 napkins of greatly different sizes (cloth works best)

Where: anywhere

How: Make up a story based on "Goldilocks and The Three Bears." Change the characters to three different-sized snowpeople who live in an ice house and who are visited by a young child. Let the action follow the original story's emphasis on large, medium, and small. As you tell the story, use the cutouts and incorporate the props into the story. Place the largest items with the largest snowperson, the medium-sized items with the medium-sized snowperson, and the smallest items with the smallest snowperson. Let the children help tell the story, and encourage them to embellish it. Place all of the props in the Language Area or the Dramatic Play Area so children can play with them and sort them by size.

Variations:
Make up other size stories using characters that match the season—birds, chicks, bunnies, reindeer, sled dogs, penguins, or turkeys, for example.

This activity helps children learn about:
sorting, matching, adapting stories, and creative thinking.

Sticker Patterns
A Quick Trick with Stickers

Gather These Materials:
20 index cards
many stickers of the same theme (for example, dinosaurs)
clear, adhesive-backed paper

Where: anywhere

How: On each of 10 index cards stick one sticker. Stick two stickers on each of the remaining cards. Demonstrate to the children how to make a simple A-B-A-B pattern with the cards showing one dinosaur, two dinosaurs, one dinosaur, two dinosaurs. Encourage the children to use the cards to make this pattern. Place the cards where children can use them when they desire.

Variation:
Make additional cards with three stickers on each card. Demonstrate using all of the cards to form an A-B-C-A-B-C pattern and encourage children to do the same.

This activity helps children learn about:
recognizing and making patterns and predicting what comes next.

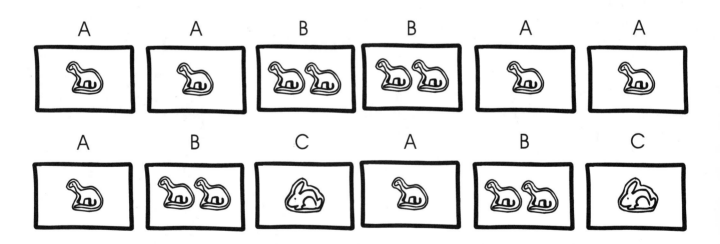

Quick Tricks for Learning ©2001 Monday Morning Books, Inc.

These Go Together
A Quick Trick with Magnetic Numbers and Letters

Gather These Materials:
a variety of magnetic letters
a variety of magnetic numbers

Where: at a magnetic surface

How: Working with one child or a small group of children, demonstrate how to stick the magnetic letters to a magnetic surface. Use a refrigerator door, the side of a file cabinet, a steel cookie sheet, or an oil drip pan. Invite the children to sort the letters by color. Later, suggest they sort these into two groups and have them select the criterion. If they can't think of a criterion suggest that they put curvy letters in one place and straight letters in another. Later, they might find the letters that begin their own and their friends' names and put all of those in one place and remaining letters in another. Always talk with them about what they've done and about the criterion they've used for sorting. Encourage all of their efforts. Repeat the activity using magnetic numbers.

Variation:
If you don't have a magnetic surface, children can sort the letters on the floor or at a table.

This activity helps children learn about:
recognizing similarities and differences, sorting, and classifying.

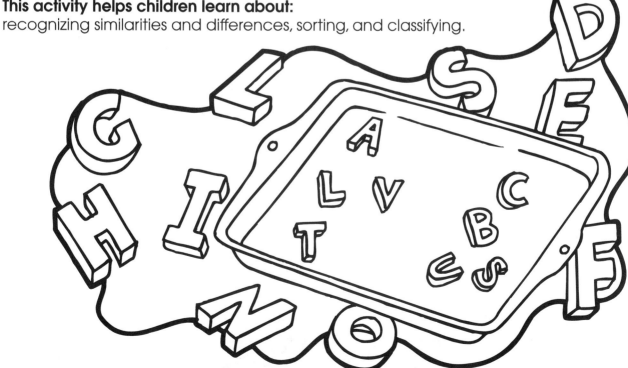

Traveling Ambassador
A Quick Trick with a Stuffed Animal

Gather These Materials:
stuffed animal of your choice
small blanket
spiral binder or other journal
pen
durable tote bag

Where: anywhere to prepare the bag
at children's homes to use the bag

How: Have children select a name for the animal. Place the selected animal, small blanket, and pen in the tote bag. On the cover of the journal, write a note to parents telling that this animal, your classroom ambassador of goodwill, has come home to spend the night with their family. The animal has brought along a blanket. Ask the family to include the bear in all of their activities that afternoon and evening, and to write in the journal, telling what the animal did during its stay. Encourage them to read aloud earlier postings from other families. Place the journal in the tote bag.

Each day, select one child to take the tote bag home. On the following day, read the family's journal entry to the entire group and choose the next child to take home the ambassador and his tote bag.

Variation:
Include an instant camera and encourage the families to take one picture of their child and the ambassador during one of their activities. Tape the photos into the journal.

This activity helps children learn about:
other children's families.

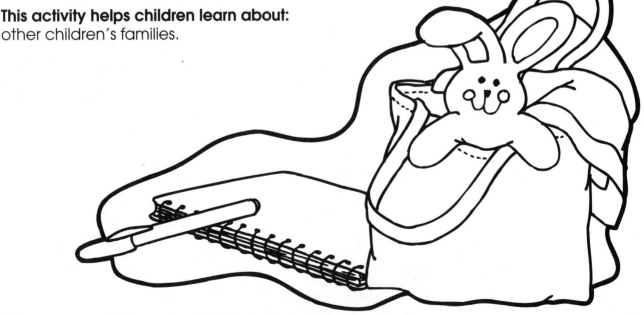

Quick Tricks for Learning ©2001 Monday Morning Books, Inc.

Squash Shapes
A Quick Trick with Winter Squash

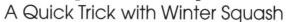

Gather These Materials:
a variety of winter squash
sharp knife (for adult use only)
tempera paint in autumn colors
sponges
pie plates
large sheets of art paper or newsprint
marker

Where: at a table

How: Gather a variety of winter squash: butternut, turban, acorn, and others that are common in your area. Show these to the large group, and pass them around so children can feel their texture and weight. Discuss the various colors, weights and textures, and the way the vegetables smell.

At a table, cut each squash vertically, from stem to bottom. Let the children handle the halves, exploring the textures and the smells.

Pour tempera paint onto sponges that are in pie plates. Use a different color for each pie plate. Have the children, in turn, select a squash half to press onto a paint-soaked sponge and then onto their papers. Let them use several different squash, and label each shape with the squash's name.

Variation:
Take photos of whole and half squash and photos of the children exploring the squash. Use the papers from the activity above as a background for a bulletin board. Place the photos on the bulletin board with captions written on sentence strips. Add pictures of the children painting with the squash, and write captions for these, too.

This activity helps children learn about:
winter vegetables, insides and outsides, and exploring with their senses.

Pattern Block Pictures
A Quick Trick with Pattern Blocks

Gather These Materials:
commercially available pattern blocks
plain paper (one or more sheets for each child)
pencil (one for each child)
markers

Where: at a table

How: Give each child a few handfuls of pattern blocks. Ask the children to create something with a few of their blocks, and then have them show their creations to each other, talking about the blocks and shapes they've used.

Give each child a sheet of plain paper and have him create a new item positioning the blocks on his paper. Show the children how to use a pencil to trace around their blocks, then have them do this. Have them remove the blocks and use markers to add color and features (eyes, teeth, ocean waves, kite string) to their tracings. If desired, have the children dictate a few sentences about their creations.

Variation:
For children who have the motor control to do this successfully, have them trace their pattern blocks onto construction paper and cut out the resulting shapes. Have them use these shapes to make pictures on their papers. Let them to use markers to add features to their creations.

This activity helps children learn about:
names of shapes, figure/ground relationships, and part/whole relationships.

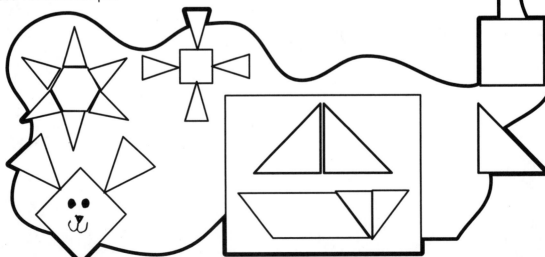

Quick Tricks for Learning ©2001 Monday Morning Books, Inc.